HOW TO BE A SUPER MAN TO YOUR WIFE

By
Jerry Humphrey

Copyright © 2007 by Jerry Humphrey

How to be a Super Man to your Wife
by Jerry Humphrey

Printed in the United States of America

ISBN 978-1-60266-899-7

All rights reserved solely by the author. The author guarantees all contents are original and do not infringe upon the legal rights of any other person or work. No part of this book may be reproduced in any form without the permission of the author. The views expressed in this book are not necessarily those of the publisher.

Unless otherwise indicated, Bible quotations are taken from the New International Version. Copyright © 1995 by Zondervan.

www.xulonpress.com

Special Thanks

All praise to my Lord and Savior Jesus Christ. I give Him special thanks for this book. Every word in this book was given to me by Him. I was just the pencil He used to write it all down.

I should like to give special thanks to my beautiful and supportive wife, Jasmine, for making this book possible. Babe, I thank you for trusting the Jesus in me to put this book into the hands of countless readers.

A special thanks to my kids: Chesarai, Chavez and Jabez for cooperating when I needed it to be silent so I could work on this book.

Purpose of this book

This book is designed to help men become better husbands to their wives. This book is fully loaded with biblical principles. The world has fed us enough lies about what a marriage should look like. It is time for truth. Only the truth sets us free and brings the fulfillment we all seek.

I have not written this book because I think I know so much about relationships or marriage, but I write because I care so much. I'll admit that I've only been married for a short time, but the only reason I decided to write this book are the for the following reasons: 1) I believe God wanted me to and 2) I really care about those who are married and want to see them restored.

Yes, this book is anchored in God's word, but Superman is the illustration I will use to convey the principles of God's word.

The first question we must ask ourselves is "What makes Superman super?" He is a hero at heart, has x-ray vision, super-hearing, can fly, leap buildings in a single bound, faster than a moving locomotive, freeze things with his breath and shoots laser beams from his eyes.

The next obvious question is what makes a husband a super man to his wife? There are qualities a husband should possess that make him super, not only from his wife's standpoint, but more importantly, from God's standpoint. A super man is a man living by God's word and principles. Let's explore them together, shall we?

Who is this book for?

This book is for Christian husbands who happen to be Superman fans. However, if you happen to be a Superman fan, but not a Christian husband – or *not even* a husband for that matter - it's cool. I'm not discriminating. Whosoever will read this book, may he/she be blessed by the contents inside.

May this book also serve as a preparatory tool to single men contemplating marriage. May this book also serve as a guiding light to the husband. May this book also be a remedy to any torn or broken marriages. If you aren't being a super man to your wife – living the Biblical role you've been called to – through the help of this book, I hope you become the super man God has called you to be.

Now a word of caution to any wives reading this book: If you and your husband are having major marital issues, I would highly recommend that you not give him this book as a gift. Please don't shove it in his face and say, "Yeah, you ought to read this so you can know how to treat me." Wives, I beg you, please don't do this. If you would say something like that to your husband, I would recommend you read *A Woman After God's Own Heart* by Elizabeth George before reading any further. However, if you wouldn't say anything like that, then read on my sister.

Now don't misunderstand me wives. You are *not* wrong for getting a hold of this book, but should you read this, "read between the lines" (see what the lesson is in it for you). A heard one pastor say, "We are not the change agents to change our spouse (husband). Only God can change our spouse."

Now with all of that being said, if you and your husband, on the other hand, happen to have a relationship "second to none," and get along with each other really well, or your husband has expressed desire to own this book, then by all means, give it to him. Otherwise, leave "well enough" alone or you risk the chance of serious backfire. And all the ladies said… _____. Remember that there are other men in your life you could give this book to if you *must* give it to someone. You could give it to an uncle, cousin, brother, nephew, etc.

Just A Guide

As I look back over my life, I recall one of my co-workers saying to me, "Jerry, the love doctor."

To all my fellow husbands, listen to me very closely. I do not consider myself to be any kind of expert in the realm of marriages or relationships. The ultimate love doctor or marriage expert is God, and He has knowledge, wisdom and understanding far beyond any doctor of medicine or doctor of theology.

I am but a mere vessel, whom God has placed His eternal treasure (His Word). I should only hope to be faithful to dispense the treasure inside of me to others. This eternal wealth is the kind of wealth to be shared with all people, and in regard to this book, eternal wealth to be shared with every husband.

I am but "a guide," not "The Guide." I am just one of many who minister on this most precious subject of marriage. Therefore, I have great respect for all my predecessors who have tackled the lies that destroy marriages around the globe. Throughout this book, I will often refer to these "modern writing prophets" who *wrote* before me. With great honor, I join them in bringing truth and healing to marriages in my generation.

Now I know this book is geared toward this particular generation, and as time passes by, and new marriage issues arise, may we always remember God's word lasts forever and will continue speaking long after I'm gone. So I say to you to extract the principles set forth in this book. Let God speak to your heart.

Withdraw the treasure inside this book deposited by God, the treasure of which was first entrusted to my heart and then deposit it into your own heart. Do this so your own marriage won't be impoverished with the world's lies, but instead rich through divine truth.

Again, don't think of me as one who has "arrived." My marriage isn't perfect either. I'm still trying everyday to get to my marital destination. We're all in this together. We're all in the same boat. All I'm doing is sharing my experiences and my heart through this book. As He is teaching me, may he teach you as well. It is said that Kix cereal is "kid-tested, mother-approved." In a similar fashion, this book is "wife-tested, Jesus-approved.

<u>One Final Word</u>

Some of you may see the word "superman" and think this book is about how to give your wife the best sex she has ever had. No, no, no my brothers. In essence, this book is about being the best husband to your wife – and doing it according to the Bible, not according to the media, Internet, or magazine articles, such as Essence or Jet.

It's unfortunate that of all men, we married men, are most miserable because our marriages lack true direction, purpose and joy. The best benefit we think of in marriage is sex. Our perspective of marriage is shallow, seeing it only as a license to have sex. Yes, what a miserable marital existence without direction, purpose and joy!

One of my goals is that we see the direction God is steering our marriages, the purpose He has for it and experience the joy too few us have really encountered.

Ephesians 5:25 says, "Husbands, love your wives, just as Christ also loved the church and gave

Himself for it." Everything I say in this book hinges completely on Scripture and its principles. I do not write this book to speak "my mind," but "His mind" about how a marriage should be. I come bearing God's truth to take back everything the devil stole from us.

For many of us, the devil has stolen our marriage. Therefore, many other things in our life are missing, such as joy, peace and fulfillment. Being robbed of the dream marriage God intended for us to have leaves us with emptiness too often experienced by most husbands. It's time to take back your marriage! Hezekiah Walker has a song that goes, "I'm reaping the harvest God promised me! Take back what the devil stole from me! And I rejoice today, for I shall recover it all!"

Recover your marriage and you will see the joy come back; you will see the peace come back and you will see the fulfillment you were always intended to have with your wife. Claim your marriage now! Your marriage is like fertile soil that needs good seeds planted in it. Then the harvest of a God-ordained matrimony will come. Let the first chapter of this book to the last be like the "rebuilding of the walls" in Nehemiah's day. As those walls were built to fortify the city of God's people, let walls of truth be rebuilt to fortify the marriage covenant between you and your wife, ordained and sanctioned by God Almighty Himself. In Jesus' name, Amen.

Now before you even begin to get into this book, let me just say that, of all men, I feel least qualified to write on such a subject as this. I realize there are many other authors, as I mentioned before, who can speak on this subject of marriage with more insight, wisdom and knowledge. If I had to choose someone to write, I would disqualify my own self. I've only been married a short time compared to some of you guys that have been married for 15 years or more. And even before getting married, I was in a previous relationship that turned really sour.

Yes, other authors come to you with multiple degrees, pastoral experience and a host of references numerous as the sand of many seashores. I come to you only in the name of the Lord. I am qualified because of He who said it to be so. This book exists only because He wills it to. As the Williams Bros. sang in their song, "I'm just a *nobody* trying to tell *everybody* about *somebody* who can save *anybody*." In this case I'd say, "I'm just a nobody trying to tell every man or husband about some truths that can save any marriage."

God has put a word in my mouth, and I must speak it. Thus, this book is here in your *hands* this very moment. May all these words that sit in your *hands* now be transferred to your <u>heart</u> so to be practiced in your life. Like M&M's, "they melt in your <u>*mouth*</u>, not in your *hands*." It is not enough to be just a listener of God's word (to read it or hear it), but a doer of His words (James 1:22). Jesus said, "Out of the overflow of your <u>heart</u>, your <u>*mouth*</u> speaks." In that context, what you speak is also what you do. Your mouth not only speaks your heart; your body *also* acts based on your heart.

So apply what you learn or else, as my former assistant pastor used to say, you will be like a dirty, unwashed man who is given a bar of soap but doesn't use it. What good is soap to a dirty unwashed man if he doesn't use it to wash himself? In the same way, how silly it would be to read this book and say, "Great book," then let it sit and collect dust for years to come. No, use the contents inside this book for your own life and marriage and then, as the Apostle Paul told Timothy, "Do the work of an evangelist," and pass it on to someone else.

Lastly, some of you may say after reading this book, "Hey, he forgot to say…" or "What about this…?" Listen, if you don't find certain subjects in this book or that the subject you are reading isn't expounded upon like you would like it to, the answers that you seek probably lie within you or in another book – perhaps another book YOU haven't written yet.

You must remember that this book isn't an encyclopedia on marriage. The focus is as the cover states, "How to be a super man to your wife." As I said before, I am one of many. No matter how detailed I would have made this book, I couldn't cover everything, but rest assured, God does have a word for you, because while I cannot say it all, God can. So listen for Him as you read this. Receive His word and let it nurture you. May it bless you richly. Amen.

Introduction: Since the Beginning

This book addresses something very critical, and too often, neglected. It addresses the painful truth husbands and most men take, and it is they believe they have no sin. This sin is called pride. To add injury to insult, there are husbands who *do* believe they have flaws and sin, but these husbands believe the sins of their wives are far greater than their own. And it is at this point, we become unbiblical, putting hierarchy on sin and making God out to be a liar when He says of Himself, "I'm no respecter of persons. I show no favoritism," and says of us, "All have sinned and come short of the glory of God."

We must realize that despite the many sins out here in the world, no sin is greater than another sin. To God, they are all the same. They all smell the same way – foul. We want God to deal with our wife, but we are just *dandy perfect*. I don't think so. We are so quick to see our wives' flaws and totally ignore our own. It would seem we take after our father – our forefather – Adam.

Think about it for a minute. When God confronted Adam and asked him, "Who told you that you were naked? Did you eat from the tree I told you not to eat from?" Adam, then responded, *"The woman You gave me* as a companion, she gave me fruit from the tree, and yes, I ate it." Does his answer sound funny to anyone else except me?

First of all, I could spend quite a time on the misconstrued confession Adam made, but let me key you in on these 5 words, "…the woman you gave me." If there weren't any problems in their marriage before the Fall, I can definitely see those problems rounding the corner to make their first appearance debut. The sadder reality is that marital sins and problems have performed "encore presentations" *since the beginning* of time up to this present age.

Now I am not claiming to know the actual problem or problems in your marriage, but one thing I do know, we husbands, must stop putting all the blame on our wives. We must stop and take a serious look in the mirror, and face the sin or sins *we do* that bring strain into our marriage. True, maybe you are not the initiator of wrong actions in your marriage, but our RE – actions are just as deadly as initiating those sins.

We have adapted what I like to call "The woman You Gave Me" mentality. This mentality shows the true nature of our hearts expressed in the pages of Jeremiah which says, "The heart is deceitful above all things…" We deceive ourselves when we won't even so much as face our *own* sin, but seek to call out every sin our wives commit.

The only truth in the comment, "the woman you gave me," which is hidden in the fabric of self – righteousness, is the acknowledgement your wife was given to you by God. Considering, then, we believe God gave our wife to us, let us explore the biblical formula for marital success.

Agree with me in prayer

Heavenly Father in the name of Jesus: may this book be a blessing to countless men all over the world, especially to those who are married. Let them know that they can have a fulfilling marriage. Let them know that's it's not too late – that You can turn it around. An angel once asked the question, "Is there anything too hard for God?" And we know the answer to that question is "No."

Let Your word of truth prevail mightily in the hearts of all who read this. Let Your word go forth like a hammer, penetrating their minds and hearts. Disarm the lies of the enemy. Through Your might, pull down the strongholds that bind us and the lies that hide us from truth. Remove the stubbornness that may lie within the heart of any reader. Don't let them be like the Pharaoh in Moses' day. Instead, in the day they hear Your voice, let them open their hearts, not harden them.

In the name of Jesus, I release every man and woman into a victorious marriage! Don't let them live a God-made institution the devil's way, but God's way. In Jesus' name I pray, Amen.

CHAPTER 1

Draw your strength from the Son:

Superman draws his strength from the sun. If Superman gets hurt really bad, in most cases, by kryptonite, he flies up toward the sun to recover his strength. We, as husbands, must do the same thing. We must draw our strength – not from the sun – but from the Son of God (Jesus Christ). In the Bible, Jesus is also referred to as the Word of God (John 1:1-3, 14). So our strength comes from God's word.

This is the most important and valuable trait a husband possesses – to depend upon God's word to govern his marriage. Praying and reading your Bible together *should be* regular maintenance for your marriage. This would also include praying regularly with your wife about your marriage. Of course, on your own devotional time with God, you ought to be praying for your marriage, too.

When you notice your marriage making a wrong turn, or feel your marriage becoming weak, fly up toward the Son, and draw your strength.

For example, maybe you notice you and your wife becoming distant toward one another. You're not communicating as much, and even when you *do* communicate, it ends up turning into an argument. In such a case, it would behoove us to address that issue (the issue of distance) immediately before it gets any worse. Before you address the issue, I would advise you to first pray by yourself, and ask God to help you see yourself, to show you where you might have gone wrong. *Yes my brothers*, you must leave open the possibility that you contributed to the issue that stands between you and your wife.

Next, approach your wife with a humble attitude. Express your heart to her about the issue and let her know you want to resolve it. Remember my brothers, not to *attack your wife* with accusations, but address the issue for peace.

You ask, "What if she doesn't agree the issue isn't a *joint* problem – that *I am* the bad guy, and she is in the right?" My answer to that is to just admit *you are* the bad guy. Remember, your initial prayer indicated you were possibly wrong, but now you want to make things right. Responding negatively or defensively to her response, should she answer this way, will only put you both back at ground zero.

Author of *The Purpose Driven Life*, Pastor Rick Warren says, "When you begin by humbly admitting your mistakes, it diffuses the other person's anger and disarms their attack because they were probably expecting you to be defensive. Don't make excuses or shift the blame; just honestly own up to any part you have played in the conflict. Accept responsibility for your mistakes and ask for forgiveness" (156-6).

So never throw blame at your wife. If she responds with this negative attitude persistently, suggest to her that you both get a third party involved, namely your local pastor, a Bible-based marriage counselor in the church you attend or a trusted friend who will not take sides. Saying such a thing will show you are serious about resolving the matter and making your marriage strong.

However, should your wife not respond negatively, which will be the case more than likely (if you come in an attitude of humility), agree, then, to pray together before talking the issue out. This is just one of the ways to "draw your strength from the Son."

COVENANT OR CONTRACT

It is very important to live your marriage "on the Rock." Today, many people have bought into the lies of the enemy (the devil) about marriage. For instance, we've been told that a marriage is "50/50." No! Marriage is 100/100. 50/50 means, "You pull your weight wife and I'll pull mine, but if you don't pull yours, I'm not pulling mine." However, 100/100 means, "I'll pull mine even if you don't pull yours." A "100/100 person" understands their role as a spouse (husband in this case) hinges only on God's word, not the wife's role. A super man focuses on his own role, and his alone.

This 50/50 mentality is one of the lies that weaken marriages. If you *have* given in to this lie, repent, and fly up toward the "Son," and draw strength for your marriage. The 100/100 mentality is the attitude you need. Ask Him for it. He'll give it to you.

Recall the words of Christ, for example. He said, "You have heard, 'An eye for an eye, and tooth for an tooth,' but I say to you, 'if someone smacks you on your right cheek, give him the other.'" Just because your wife did something wrong to you doesn't mean get back at her for it. We are to repay evil with good. It's always right to do right.

Author of *Sacred Sex*, Tim Alan Gardner states:

> Sometimes I feel as if we Americans are drowning in contracts.
>
> Whether we need an auto loan, a raise at work, or a driver's license, we're constantly putting our name on the dotted line. A contract is an arrangement between two parties whereby both sides commit to certain conditions. Inherent in the agreement is the idea that if one *side violates the terms, the other party has some type of recourse...*
>
> The provisions in a contract protect the interests of both parties.
>
> Contrast that with what happens in a wedding ceremony. Most couples seem to believe that, since both the man and the woman are asked to speak their marriage vows, they have established a contract.

In one partner's mind, that means he'll do his part as long as his spouse is doing her part (193).

Notice that Gardner speaks about the 50/50 mentality, and how it is rooted in a mind-set we are all accustomed to. I mean, obviously, we should want to protect ourselves in any kind of agreement, of course. However, the point is that he warns us, as do I, against the danger of mismatching mindsets. Keep the contract mindset with contracts and such, but keep a biblical and covenant mind-set for marriage. In other words, don't have a contract mindset for your marriage. As I said, it will weaken (like kryptonite weakens Superman) your marriage.

Part of living your biblical role or "drawing your strength from the Son" as a husband, is doing what Jesus commanded. He said, "Watch and pray. The spirit, indeed, is willing, but the flesh is weak. (Matt. 26:41) "

Often times we really concentrate on the *prayer* part of this scripture in Matt 26: 41. Don't get me wrong, prayer is powerful and *should* be done regularly (Luke 18:1; 1 Thess. 5:17). However, "watching" is equally important, and all "watching" means to do is be careful, to be cautious.

Gardner's quote above is one classic example of husbands (and wives) not being "watchful" or careful. Without realizing it, most husbands and wives have turned a God-ordained, God-sanctioned institution into a man-made organization.

I heard a pastor say, "Technology is a blessing, but it's also a curse." The reason it is a curse is due to the kind of attitude and mentality is *can* create – attitudes and mentalities that are not conducive to a life of godliness.

For example, it's not wrong to have DSL on your computer. DSL is a wonderful technological breakthrough, and offers Internet speed at high volumes for the Internet surfer. However, it is easy to "get used to" the speed DSL offers, and begin to subconsciously think God should operate the same way. At the click of our fingers or at our command, we may start to think if God doesn't respond like the DSL on our computers, He must not be God or He is not being the puppet God we want Him to be.

The danger of mismatching mindsets is that we begin comparing God to the DSL, instead of comparing the DSL to God. And God is greater than the DSL.

Here is another example. I heard the story of a police officer that treated his wife just like his job. He brought his militant-mentality and attitude home to his wife, which was appropriate for his police job, but completely inappropriate for his marriage. Do you see the danger that I speak of?

Some of you may remember the movie *The Gospel*. In the movie, a preacher named Frank told his wife Charlene, "Baby, you're not the congregation…you're my wife." Wanting to be sexually intimate with his wife (but she didn't want to be intimate with him), he said this to her in mild frustration. The notion he was making was that there is a time and place for his preacher mentality. At home with his wife was not the place. He could "get busy" with his wife, but not the church, if you will.

So the 50/50 mindset is good for a business transaction or loan program, but not for your marriage.

The truth is some of us live our lives as policemen, work with computers all day or do some activities that require certain types of mind-sets, which for whatever those activities, are fine. However, for your marriage, an appropriate mind-set is well in order and very much needed for its survival.

This is why I suggest we stay in God's word, reading it everyday. The 100/100 mindset is bottled in reading and studying the word of God. Also surround yourself with godly people and anything that's godly. Let your entire being be infiltrated with the principles of God's word.

I know people who keep scriptures posted all over their house or their car. You name it and it's there. You may say, "Aw, that's baby Christian stuff – putting scriptures all over the place." Not necessarily. If you stay around God all day, you can't help but act the way He acts or wants you to live your life.

That "baby Christian stuff," as some call it, will be the lifeline for your marriage! The truth be told, that "baby Christian stuff" isn't really baby stuff; it is the spiritual sustenance needed for every believer to do God's will. God's will in this case being your marriage.

The Bible says to "guard your heart with all diligence." Yes, even the little things that aren't, per se, sins, we must watch out for any way. Recall the scripture that says, 'Lay aside everything that slows us down from spiritual progression and the sin, which so easily entangles us. (Hebrews 12:1)" The devil is attacking us from every angle. He knows our spirits (our hearts) are like sponges, soaking up the environment around it. He seeks to plant evil in our hearts, so we must guard it with our very lives. Our life actually *does* depend on it.

The thing about the enemy is that he also knows we were born in sin, and knows we are inclined to do wrong and sinful things. He knows all he has to do is set traps for us and let us be enticed and led away of our own lusts. This is why it is important to stay "in the book" – God's word. The devil has traps set up every where, even in places you'd think he'd never put them. It's impossible to know his every move, but God has given us a sure weapon to be prepared for every snare – that weapon being His word.

Notice in the movie *Superman Returns*, Superman doesn't just fly up toward the sun to draw strength only in the time of *need*, but he flew up there everyday to stay strong. If he didn't do it regularly, he wouldn't be able to do all the things he could do…you know… such as stopping bullets with his own body, picking up large buildings without a sweat, etc. In the same way, you will never have a strong, lasting marriage if you don't stay in the word of God.

Every day, draw your strength from the "Son," and your marriage will "withstand all the wicked wiles (tricks) of the evil one. (Ephesians 6:13)"

CHAPTER 2

Use your X-ray Vision

Now allow me to clarify this X-ray Vision concept for anyone thinking what I *think* you're thinking. It is <u>not</u> using your imagination trying to see through *other women's* clothes or your wife's. *However, thinking sexually about your wife is okay.* As far as other women go, though, it is forbidden. "Undressing other women with your eyes" is completely inappropriate. Some of the common things men say in movies (and real life) are "What color panties is she wearing?" Or worse, trying to imagine other women naked. According to Matthew 5: 32, doing the things I just mentioned are adultery and lusting…and both are sins.

You may say, as most men usually say, "There ain't no harm in looking," or "There's nothing wrong with looking." This sounds innocent enough, but consider King David. For him, "harmless" looking turned into lusting; lusting led to sex; sex led to an unexpected pregnancy; unexpected pregnancy led to a cover-up scam; a cover-up scam led to conspiracy to murder...well, I think you get the point. (Check out 2 Samuel 11).

Just as there is a thin line between love and hate, there is a thin line between harmLESS and harmFUL, especially when it comes to being a married man trying to remain faithful (sexually exclusive to his wife only). Even "single" Christians need to watch their "wandering eyes." Yes, it's true that Christian singles don't have wives to be faithful to, but are still called to sexual purity. At least when you *do* decide to marry, you will be sexually pure! Be faithful to the wife you haven't even met yet.

If *harmless looking* can turn into *harmful repercussions* as it happened to David, it can happen to us, too. As the Bible says, "Don't be so naïve and self-confident. You're not exempt. You could fall flat on your face as easily as anyone else" (1 Corinthians 10:12 *The Message Bible*).

I mean, you wouldn't like it if your wife thought sexually about other men. Wouldn't you feel betrayed? Of course you would. Now there are a lot of these so-called men out there who do everything "under the sun" in regard to being unfaithful to their wives. They flirt with other women. They visit strip bars or pay for sex. They have women on stand-by (some of us better know this as having "the little black book" – a book filled with women's addresses, phone numbers and even their e-mail just in case their marriage isn't doing that great. It is the unofficial "sexually driven" prenuptial agreement! They call these women up for a "booty call," a.k.a. a sexual encounter) and we have men who view porn on a daily basis thinking, "What is the harm? I'm not going to do anything with these women." Maybe not, but that doesn't mean your wife won't feel betrayed! And on and on it goes.

I've known men who, upon finding out their wife (or significant other S.O.) cheated on them (yet they are cheating on their wives or S.O.), were completely devastated. They were so hurt and basically pledged in their heart to leave her. They wanted to end the relationship. Meanwhile, they themselves justified their affairs, but her affair was unacceptable. This is pure hypocrisy! *No*, she isn't allowed to have affairs either, but why is it okay for men to do it? Like I said…HYPOCRISY…and might I add, selfishness.

Such loose living is one example of what the Bible calls, "lovers of pleasure more than lovers of God" (2 Timothy 3:4). If we loved God, we wouldn't betray our wife in this way – not the woman to whom we pledged unfailing love.

Dr. Jimmy Evans calls this *feeling* of betrayal "legitimate jealousy." She is exclusively for you, and no one else. You are entitled to *feel* a little jealous if she were to show interest in another man. Now I'm not encouraging any of us to *choose* to be jealous and what the Bible calls sin. *Feeling* jealous and *being* jealous are two different things. Let me explain.

To <u>not</u> *feel* jealousy when you wife purposely thinks of other men sexually, or flirts with them is questionable. The question I would ask such a man who had no feeling of betrayal or legitimate jealousy is "Do you even love your wife?" It isn't natural to <u>not</u> feel betrayed if you knew your wife purposely did this. That feeling of betrayal is called legitimate jealousy (it's okay to feel betrayed).

Legitimate jealousy is a human response, not a sinful one. I mean, didn't Judas Iscariot betray Jesus for 30 shekels of silver? Jesus even knew before Judas betrayed Him that he would *actually* betray Him. Of course, Jesus would have preferred Judas to love Him more than the money he betrayed him for, but notice that Jesus never <u>*reacted sinfully*</u> toward Judas for betraying him! My brothers, if Jesus could *experience* betrayal and not respond in sin, we can do the same.

God even says, "I am a jealous God." By right, we belong to God and Him alone. When we put other things or people before Him, He is jealous. We know God to be holy and perfect. His jealousy is legitimate. He is well within His rights to be jealous. Worship belongs to God alone. As is said in Christian circles, "God doesn't share His *glory* with any body." In the same way sexually, whether in deed, thought or word, we *only* give ourselves to our wives. Period! So don't be surprised if your wife doesn't want you to share "your sexual glory" with another, or it could very well become a *gory story*, if you catch my drift. More importantly, God has reserved your sexual glory for your wife and hers for you.

However, "*being* jealous" is an act of your own will, (the kind the Bible forbids – a sinful response). It is a harmless emotional response exchanged for harmful sinful acts, such as treating your wife the same way by flirting with other women or reacting sinfully or violently (you know…a domestic case where police get involved).

However, don't get it twisted! I'm not endorsing responses of pettiness, violence or domestic disturbances for any jealous *feelings*, or even if you are tempted to actually be jealous (in a sinful way), but if we can be legitimately jealous, aren't our wives entitled just the same? *I rest my case*. And now that I've explained what X-Ray Vision is not, let us get to what it is.

HONOR HER BODY AND SPIRIT

Superman could see through walls. As husbands, we are called to see her physical beauty, yet at the same time we are to look past or through her external beauty to see her inner beauty. Needless to say, she is more than a physical being, right? She is spiritual and emotional, too. We must see the beauty of these spiritual and emotional aspects of her as well.

The Bible says, "There are husbands who, indifferent as they are to any words about God, will be captivated by your life of "holy beauty." What matters is not your outer appearance – the styling of your hair, the jewelry you wear, the cut of your clothes – but your inner disposition. Cultivate inner beauty, the gentle, gracious kind that God delights in." (1 Peter 3:1-4 *The Message Bible*).

Notice the words, "holy beauty," "inner disposition," and "inner beauty." Now I know this passage is teaching wives how to be the biblical wife they are called to be to their husbands. However, use your "holy" imagination for a moment and see past the "way she is called to live as a wife," and see the concept being taught here for us husbands.

THOU SHALT NOT COVET THY WIFE'S BODY

Now as husbands, we sometimes allow the fact we are *physically stimulated* get the best of us at times. Don't get me wrong, if your wife turns you on, that's great! The Bible tells us in the book of Proverbs, "may her breasts satisfy you," and Song of Solomon says, "may your breasts be like clusters on the vine…and your mouth like the best wine." However, like "Transformers, robots in disguise" there is more to her than what you can actually see. If you only see that aspect of her, you are in for a rude awakening. She isn't just some sex object to "get off" on. Sex is only one of the vital elements needed in your marriage to make it work. Remember that her body is the temple of the Holy Spirit, not the temple for all of your crazy erotic sexual fantasies.

The unfortunate tragedy today is that we live in a world that worships butts and breasts, hips and thighs, and of course the obvious one. (Come on guys, don't make me say it). Coveting after these things not only are covetous and degrading of women, but idolatrous. Shrines and temples haven't been erected with female body parts made of stone and gold and such, but our culture *has built* new shrines to the ancient sex goddess Aphrodite.

Today, the many names she goes by are Porn and Pimpin,' just to name a few. For a striptease in special clubs for men, the many men who go bring hundreds of dollars funding the survival of such institutions. And these are men who aren't just single men, but men who have wives at home.

GO 'HEAD WITH YOUR HOLY SELF

Now let's turn our attention from physical beauty to "holy beauty," "inner disposition," and "inner beauty." Is your wife saved? Does she have a personal relationship with Jesus? Does she live for God? If the answer is yes, know that this is a beautiful thing. Some of us men will never become super men to our wives because we resent her relationship with God – who, by the way, is our God, too. She is supposed to put Him before you. I mean, hey, it is God who put you two together to begin with, right?

God the Father is not the same as your wife's *earthly* father. Earthly fathers give away their daughters to their husbands, meaning the husbands now have priority over the father of the bride (Gen. 2:24). However, when Our Heavenly Father gave us our wife, He still has priority over us. He still comes first.

Again, don't get me wrong, if your wife is giving it all to God, and not paying you a lick of attention, that is sinful and unbiblical – that is an issue that needs to be handled immediately. (Now, let me say, just before you go off on the deep end and go *tell your wife about herself*, consider yourself first. Perhaps, you, as the husband, have not put your wife in her proper place – "first place" in your life *under* God. Maybe you've been putting sports and TV before her. Check yourself before you wreck yourself and your marriage. Don't be so quick to judge her. Judge yourself).

Next, let's take a look at her emotional side. Another thing we husbands don't do is praise and compliment our wives enough, if we do it at all. Remember... marriage isn't self-maintained. It is not a blind effort that just happens to work if the sun is shining on the right day. It takes a conscious effort being married to bring desired results – you know... joy, peace, and fulfillment.

Psalm 22:3 says, "God lives in the praises of His people." There is something special about praise. Even God himself gravitates toward those who praise Him.

One cliché says, "When praises go up, blessings come down." A woman, or your wife, isn't any different. She literally lives in the praises of her husband. If you send her genuine praise – not flattery (false compliments for your own selfish reasons – like for sex), she will honor you with her presence. So let us conclude: when praises go forth, intimacy springs up.

Now by "her presence," I don't just mean your wife being around you, but the two of you experiencing intimacy on levels far above your wildest imagination.

Very briefly, let me explain intimacy. Intimacy doesn't mean *just* sex, but experiencing a oneness together on a multitude of levels. Your communication is one outcome that may get better "on point" (verbal intimacy). Your ability to share intimate things about each other will probably be one door to open up (emotional intimacy), or your trust level may heighten to heights unimaginable. Whatever it is my brothers, rest assured, you'd experience something good and almost indescribable with your wife.

Once again, look past the text itself, and let us see the lesson in it for us. As a woman uses lipstick to enhance her physical beauty, we husbands, should wear praise on our lips everyday to enhance the beauty or "the handsomeness" of who we are. Let praise be the make-up you wear. Your wife will think you are stunning and handsome. Psalm 34:1 says, "I will bless the Lord at all times, and His praises shall continually be in my mouth." May husbands say this very same thing of their wives: I will praise my wife at all times. Her praises shall continually be in my mouth.

Now for some husbands, who didn't quite get what I said about praise being on our lips, let me clarify. There is no such thing as praise lipstick for men or houses built of praise (lol). All I mean by those analogies are to praise and compliment your wife everyday.

The best home you can give your wife is a *home of praise*. Now you can be rich and buy her the biggest house with 8 big bedrooms, 2 bathrooms with one in the master bedroom, walk-in closet, etc., but if you do not praise her, it is all for nothing – it's worthless. Dr. Jimmy Evans said in his book, *Marriage on the Rock*, "A woman blossoms fully in an atmosphere of praise and adoration, but she wilts and dies in the presence of silence or criticism…[They] naturally gravitate to people and places where they will receive compliments about themselves."

LOVE & PRAISE: MARRIAGE TAG TEAM CHAMPIONS

1 Corinthians 13:5 reads, "…[Love] keeps no record of wrongs." One way you know you truly love someone is if you don't hold their past sins against you against them. You don't brew it in your mind and heart over and over again, reliving the hurt and the pain. Even if the person who wronged you *wrongs* you again, you don't take the opportunity to throw past sins they've done to you in their face.

Okay, where am I going with this, you ask? Here's where I'm going. In order *not* to record wrongs done to us by our wives in our hearts, we need to do the exact opposite of keeping "wrong records." We need to keep "right records," and not only keep the record in our hearts, but to actually put it down on paper, too.

The problem today is that we don't seem to remember all the nice, generous and kind things our wives have done for us. It would seem all the bad things stick in our minds for almost an eternity. We hold grudges, bottle up pain, and preserve offenses that rob us of our God-given joy and peace.

So when we truly _love_ our wives, _praise_ will follow our love. Even in those times when the two of you are in disagreement or aren't seeing eye to eye, having all the good and nice things she does down on paper, or in a journal, will help bring you back to focus. You will focus on the fact she was given to you by God and tremendously help diffuse any of your unkind thoughts or anger on the verge of becoming sinful.

So here is what I want you to do. On the next page, you will find a one-page journal in which you will fill with nice, loving, kind and "right" actions your wife has ever done to you. Write two or three praises in it every week, and review it every week, too. Especially use this when the two of you are working each other's last nerves. Doing this exercise will help you even to give your wife regular compliments.

How to be a Super Man to your Wife

Now I will say one last thing of praising and complimenting your wife. Most of us are familiar with Proverbs 31. It speaks of the virtuous woman, or the ideal wife every man desires. It lists all her virtuous good qualities. Any way, let's take this scripture and apply it to our lives as husbands. Prov. 31:28 says, "[Her] husband joins in with words of praise." So if Proverbs 31 shows the *ideal woman*, it is equally true that *praise* is the *ideal* action of every husband. So let every husband that has breath praise ye his wife!"

Now here are two more classic church cliches to help us understand the importance of praising our wives. This cliché goes, "Count your blessings. You'll be amazed," and the other one says, "When I think of the goodness of Jesus, and all He's done for me, my very soul cries out Hallelujah! Thank God for saving me."

So count the many times your wife has blessed you, whether it be her cooking you dinner or breakfast, washed your clothes, bought you that special gadget for the car you've been wanting, buying lingerie, etc. Count them and you will be amazed. You'll realize that she is more wonderful than you remember.

Now the key phrase in the second cliché is "think of the goodness." We must *think of the goodness* our wives have done for us, even in the midst of her getting on our nerves, or when we aren't exactly happy with her. Maybe the two of you just had a disagreement. Go into your time-out area, cool off and start thinking of all the good things she has done for you to keep the disagreement simply that - a disagreement - and not allow it to escalate to what has been known as "intense fellowship" (arguing and fighting).

The Apostle Paul even said to us from the pages of Philippians 4:8. "Summing it all up friends, I'd say you'll do best by filling your minds and meditating on things true, noble, reputable, authentic, compelling, gracious – the best, not the worst; the beautiful, not the ugly; things to praise, not things to curse."

I know. You're probably saying, this scripture in Phil. 4:8 isn't talking about praising my wife. And you're right. It doesn't say that *exactly*. However, the principle *to praise* your wife is woven in this scripture. Don't focus on the bad things she does, and I put emphasis on the word *focus*. Focusing on the negative tends to make you negative *and* your marriage, but focusing on the positive tends to make you positive *and* your marriage. I'm not insisting ignoring flaws and healthy confrontation, but marital problems arise when the focus is on "the bad, the worst and the ugliest."

Nasty arguments between a wife and husband are tricks of the devil, and the devil has branded us with statements that "all couples *fight*." He has made us believe this is true but it isn't. Arguments, actually start off as emotional spurts, but later are chosen by our own wills to *keep* arguing, producing an end result of some type or types of violence, be it verbal, sexual or physical. The initial disagreement or fight diffuses after a moment, but is kept alive by the participants – you and your wife. At this point, your marriage is at-risk of becoming dangerous and unhealthy. And

God help us if we have children who are spectators of our "intense fellowship."

Arguments! We all know about arguments. Many of us as children bear the mark of coming up in homes where arguments/fights between our parents happened regularly. We remember the shouting, the "bad words," door slams, and the walkouts. I mean, it was verbal abuse at its peak. What made these arguments so bad, more than anything, were the after effects. We remember the discomfort of just wanting to run away so we could have peace *or* jumping in the middle of the argument – not really knowing what to do, but it sure beat doing nothing at all.

Despite these nasty fights our parents would get into, some of the things they would say to each other were *actually* true. You may be asking, "What's so true about mom saying to dad, 'I can't stand you. You make me sick!'"

Well, think about it for a moment. As our parents would go back and forth, the kind of truth that was exchanged is what I call "brutal honesty." This kind of honesty is never appropriate. This honesty is out of control, where our total emotional make-up (in most cases, anger) is like a pinball in a pinball machine – it's everywhere. Arguments are spoken truths outside the bounds of appropriate timing, respect and sensitivity of one another. Outside these bounds lie pure selfishness.

Some of us say, "I would never argue to the point of being brutally honest." Then there are others among us who say, "I've never argued to the point of disrespecting my wife." I advise caution not to think of ourselves above such actions and words. So for those of us that *have* been down the road of being brutally honest, let me say this: there are not too many people that know our spouses better than we do. We know what they *can* do and *cannot* do. We know things about our wives no one else knows. We got the 4-1-1 on our wives! This 4-1-1, or all we know of our wives, is ground for a healthy marriage, but we use the 4-1-1 for badgering our wife, producing just the opposite of a healthy marriage. The more we know of her, the more responsible we are to treat her with all the decency, respect, courtesy and love we have.

Since it is true we know more of our wives than anybody else, why is it we have the most difficulty with this woman we call "wife?" The other painful truth is that many of us gloat of how much we know our wives – of how we know her ways. Instead of gloating and complaining, we ought to be accommodating our knowledge of her. What do I mean by this? I mean simply this: Don't praise yourself for knowing your wife, and then do nothing but complain about how she is. Considering what you know, always be conscientious of her ways and adjust your own attitude and actions to keep the peace between the both of you as God intended (1 Peter 3:7). This is what I call the *catering principle*.

Remember not to compromise with your wife to the point of making yourself uncomfortable. Compromise or cater to her within reasonable limits. Yes, there is "give and take" in marriage, but too much of either will put a strain on your marriage. There is healthy and unhealthy catering or compromise.

There are times you will have to respectfully draw the line in the sand, but then other times, you will have to reevaluate yourself and make some changes for the peace and survival of your marriage. If you don't compromise healthily, you will only heap more problems upon the ones that already exist.

So what do you think I am supposing will happen here in Phil 4:8 if we obey it? Just the opposite my brothers – not marital turmoil – peace. Praise your wife and you will be at-risk for world peace in your home.

Instead of giving sexual praises like, "Baby, you look sexy in that outfit," focus in on something about her character; how she handles the children, or how committed she is to crafting, writing, fitting in well in new settings. Whatever it is, let her know you see her and *all* that she is and does.

CHAPTER 3

Be a Man of Steal, Not a Man of Steel

One of the things that made Superman so cool was that virtually nothing could hurt him. Thus, he became known as the "Man of Steel." Shooting him didn't affect him. The bullets just reflected off of him like a kid bouncing on a trampoline.

However, for us husbands, being "men of steel," is a character quality we *do not* want to have. I'm not saying we shouldn't be physically strong and equipped to protect our wife (or children) from physical harm. By all means, be in-shape, and exercise regularly.

Instead, in this chapter I especially write for you husbands who struggle expressing affection to your wife and opening your heart to her, or you husbands who want to be "Mr. Tough Guy," all the time. Don't get me wrong. Be "Mr. Tough Guy," but realize that there is a time and place to be "Mr. Tough Guy," but with your wife, be "Mr. Affection."

So when I say "men of steel," I mean husbands who are almost emotionless, or men who don't express their feelings. Because we've been geared to be strong (yet misunderstood the true essence of strength) we think not sharing our weak moments, fears, failures or affection (love on contact) with our wives is the way to maintain this strength. We think that at the moments we share all these things, we become weak.

Many of us get caught up with the idea that women (or our wives) want a "buff" man with bulging muscles who doesn't have any fears, zero failures, always has money, gives hours and hours of great orgasmic sex and doesn't feel any pain. Now I understand there are women out in the world who want the kind of man I just described, but they are just as deluded as the man who thinks "invincibility" is the key to a great marriage.

See my brothers, after you have stopped a moving locomotive with your bare hands and rise completely refreshed from multiple hours of non-stop sex, your wife still needs a husband who feels pain and shares them with her. Even the Terminator, though he could not *feel* pain, had a "pain sensory chip" located in its metallic skull. She still needs you to touch her without becoming sexual, and she still needs affectionate remarks for absolutely no reason at all.

AFFECTION: A GIRL'S BEST FRIEND

Now allow me to just reiterate that men showing affection isn't a sign of weakness. The world would have us believe a man being sentimental or affectionate to his wife is "sissy-ism." Nothing could be further from the truth!

You know, intuitively or deep down inside, that if you were to be affectionate to your wife, you would receive a pleasant response or reaction from her.

Now just to quickly clarify what affection is, I mean things like holding hands, caressing her arm or face, or even telling her verbally that you love her, and not allow it to become sexual or do it so it can lead to sex ultimately. Funny, we know to do these things, but we do not. Why? The answer is as I said before. The world, which is a product of Satan's lies, told us it is weak for men to be affectionate.

THOU SHALT NOT BEAR FALSE WITNESS FROM THY WORLDLY NEIGHBORS

Look at this. The lie that men shouldn't be affectionate is not only a lie, but also a curse. For some of us who have bought this lie have cursed our marriages before we ever said, "I do." Unaware, of course, most of us were deceived by this cursed lie. Many of us were taught as young boys that affection is a "no-no."

Many of us learned <u>not</u> to be affectionate because our fathers never were to our moms or even to us. Another majority of us never even had a male role model present to show real, genuine affection. The best male role models we ever had came from TV. Sometimes our role models came from the streets where we might have overheard (way too often, I might add) glimpses of them talking about body parts of a woman like they were toys you could play with if you said the right stuff to her (mackin,' they call it).

When we liked a girl in school, for instance, we didn't just come up to her and say "I like you, would you like to be my girlfriend?" No, instead, we playfully hit her or smacked her "where the sun don't shine." We taunted and teased her with our other male compradres. We showed we liked her without letting everyone *else* know we did, but the crazy truth is that despite the hitting and teasing, everyone *still* knew we liked her.

Now while the girl in grade school (assuming she isn't your wife today) was not your wife, and such behavior among children was normal back then – and still is today in schools all over the world– the absence of affection is *deadly* to all marriages.

Unfortunately, the lie is implanted in many of us before we even reach those critical pre-teen years, where we began liking girls. For most of us, our natural inclination to like girls was poisoned before we reached the age of 10, if not earlier.

LOVE ON CONTACT

I mentioned earlier in chapter 2 that our wives gravitate toward praise. Well…they also gravitate toward *affection*. Author and pastor Dr. Jimmy Evans said in his book, "...Non-sexual touching (Affection) is a major need in a woman...If you don't normally touch and caress your wife in soft, non-sexual ways, you need to begin to do that. Regardless of your past or present dislikes, it fulfills and satisfies an extremely important need in your wife's life." To say the least, affection validates your wife as a person. She needs to know she is *more* than some *sexual excursion*. It tells her you care for her deeply. It helps make her secure in your love for her and that she is the only woman *you* want to be with forever.

If I may, allow me to use a few illustrations to stress the necessity of affection to one's wife. There is an old classic movie I love called *The Thornbirds*, a 4-part movie series. In the 3rd part, a man named Luke O'Neil married a young lady, Megan Cleary. In the very beginning of their marriage, he was sweet and gentle to her. Soon after their honeymoon, he got a job working in a field making a lot of money. The job required many, many hours of work and would require him to be away from his wife one week at a time. So he arranged for her to stay with some good, decent people until the two of them could get settled. By this time, they still had not settled in a home of their own.

NO HITTING BELOW HER WAIST

Soon, the first day of work began for Luke. As he was hopping in the truck with his new work buddies, he leaned in to kiss his wife good-bye, but then all his soon-to-be fellow co-workers started taunting him and mumbly cheered him *not* to kiss his own wife. Do you believe that? His own wife! Well, Luke *didn't* kiss his wife. So instead of giving her that kiss of affection, he jumped back into macho-mode, the bachelor-mentality and smacked her on the behind. You could almost imagine the look she gave him and how degraded she felt about that unexpected slap to the rear.

As we can see, he loved his friends more than his own wife! In such cases, for most men like Luke, a wife is nothing more than a convenience - just for sex or a trophy wife who's only there to make them look good. See how he thought affection meant weakness and that he wasn't a "real" man, but little do we know that affection is a demonstration of strength. It keeps our marriages strong and healthy while the absence of it, will leave our marriages weak and unfulfilling. As I mentioned in chapter one, when your marriage gets weak, (or in order to maintain its strength) you need to *draw* your strength from the Son.

Such men who withdraw affection resemble many ancient kings. For ancient kings, their love of power extended far beyond politics, conquering other kingdoms and expanding their empires. Their love of power extended to their very own bedrooms. Their wives became the objects for their sexual urges.

Some of you remember the other classic movie, *The 10 Commandments,* where Charlton Heston played the part of Moses. In the movie, Pharaoh (Ramses) told his soon-to-be-wife, and I quote, "You will be my wife. You will come to me whenever I call you." This is a reference to sex, but notice the absence of affection. These kings were living the popular classic song by Tina Turner, "What's love got to do with it," long before it became a hit sensation in the 1980's or even a song.

Unfortunately, many of us husbands today are still living the 1980 hit sensation, *What's love got to do with it* with our wives. What's affection got to do with it? We ask. "There is no need for affection" is what we actually are saying. "As long as I bring home the 'bread,' that is all she needs," we say. We have to know that refusing to express affection to our wives is an "matrimonial album flop," and certainly not a hit!

HEAVENLY AFFECTION

Don't think for a minute that affection, which is a form of love, is weak. It is much stronger than you can possibly imagine! Just think of the goodness of Jesus and His death for us on the cross. That was love! Think of all the times that God reassured you He loved you – be it by His word or His presence. He even gave us Communion to remind us of His love for us! My friend, that's "heavenly" affection! Let Jesus be your example of affection. Yes, He is our Chief Priest, but He is also our Chief Example of love and affection. The Bible even tells husbands to love their wives as *Christ* loved the church.

Speaking of Jesus, let's look at Matthew 13:1-8, 18-23, the parable of the sower/farmer. I encourage you to read the entire passage on your own, but I would like to focus on "the seeds that fell among thorns and were choked out."

As we know, Jesus taught the different ways people respond to the message of the kingdom of God. The seed that fell among thorns represents people who are too concerned with the things this world has to offer. They'd rather have death rather than life. They'd rather have a life aimed at pleasure instead of a life aimed at pleasing God. As Jesus said in another place, "They loved darkness rather than light because their deeds were evil."

Some of us are too concerned about worldly principles that are destroying our marriages every day, than to hear the word of truth that can save it. Those worldly principles are choking the life out of our marriages. For example, God created sex for oneness in marriage, but the world took sex and made a monster out of it. The world teaches us to use it like a recreational activity like sports or leisure activities. We need to cut out the weeds of worldly principles (which are lies or kryponite for our marriages) so our marriages can grow to their greatest potential – blessing our lives, our marriages and those around us. We can't live biblical marriages according to the world's standards.

TOUCHED BY A HUSBAND

Now to avoid the lie or marital kryponite of absentee affection, let me tell you what kind of man we should be. We should be "Men of Steal." Notice the word *steal* as opposed to *steel*. "Men of steal" are men who sweep their wives off their feet; they are romantic; men who share their feelings, whether it be fears, weaknesses and failures, or successes and triumphs; men who are gentle, affectionate and sensitive, but can balance it with toughness. They can get in touch with their *feminine side* (if you will) and yet be *masculine*.

Now I am in no way pushing or promoting homosexuality by saying *getting in touch with our feminine side*. Neither am I pushing weakness or sissy-ism, as I just established only a few paragraphs ago. Even Jesus wept, the Bible says (St. John 11:35).

Now the idea behind "getting in touch with our feminine side" means taking on a characteristic *women* tend to be like. And women tend to be affectionate, nurturing, caring, sensitive and gentle. As I said earlier, a wife gravitates toward her husband when he is affectionate to her.

In essence, *men of steal* steal the heart of their wives. You know the expression most women say is "He stole my heart?" Well, this is one of the moves we need to be making on our wives. Everyday let us win the heart of our wives. Constantly we are to let her know how special she is to us.

There is a song by the late Reverend James Cleveland that goes like this: *Give me my flowers right now while I yet live so I can see the beauty of them.* The concept, of course, is that one cannot enjoy the flowers dead. Of course, "flowers" in this song refer to nice compliments, praise, or celebrating someone with heartfelt words and expression that we would usually render at their funeral. In the same way, we shouldn't wait until our wife is dead (or if our marriage is dead) and gone to let her know how special she is to us.

AS A MATTER OF FACT, GO AND TELL HER RIGHT NOW. SERIOUSLY, MY BROTHERS, STOP READING THIS BOOK FOR A MOMENT AND GO TELL HER HOW MUCH SHE MEANS TO YOU. EVEN IF YOU NEED TO TAKE A FEW MINUTES TO THINK OR WRITE DOWN WHY SHE IS IMPORTANT TO YOU AND ALTOGETHER LOVELY, DO IT. THEN, CARESS HER ARM GENTLY, LOOK INTO HER EYES AND THEN KISS HER ON THE CHEEK…GO RIGHT NOW)… Now that you're back… That wasn't so hard, now was it? Don't worry, though. Make it a regular practice, and it will become like breathing and NO JOKE, you will become a "real life" super man!

ALL THAT SHE WANTS

Now let's go back to that movie I love so much, *ThornBirds*. There was a woman in the movie married to a man for many years. All their marriage, he showed her affection, but she never showed him any. Later, he died in a forest fire. A priest, a friend of their family, did his funeral. Afterward, the wife of her deceased husband talked to the priest and in tears expressed how much she had loved her husband. She said sobbing, "All he ever wanted me to say to him was that I loved him…I do love him, father!" This woman in the movie wasn't the emotional type, which made it twice as hard for her to show her husband affection.

She gave her husband his "flowers" all right, but he was dead when she finally did. Such things need to be said, husbands, while your wife yet lives. Give them to her while you can see her reaction – you know, the expression on her face or how her eyes dance to your love song.

Husbands, the only thing (or one of the things) your wife wants you to do is tell her you love her. We need to show it as well. She needs to know you can *feel*. We can't afford to NOT be the emotional type. We need to blend that emotional type into the very core of who we are.

I, myself, am not the emotional type. I find that I have to purposely show affection to my wife. I am naturally a serious person, logical and analytical. These traits leave little room for emotion. I make it up in my mind to be affectionate to her. One of the things that help me show affection to my wife are those little nudges from God…you know…those ideas that seem like regular, random ideas out of thin air.

Did you ever get a crazy idea, for example, to write down 7 compliments or ways to show affection to your wife for an entire week? Or did you ever have an idea to massage her neck right after dinner? My brothers, those little "so-called" insignificant ideas are more God-centered ideas than we think. Just listen. God often speaks in a still small voice and through normal every day occurrences. God may not speak an exact scripture to our heart, but He always speaks the principles of His word to our hearts.

One idea I had (and this was before my wife and I married) was to give her scripture and compliments by mail. One time I even threw in a pita-colada scent in the envelope. She loved it. I couldn't see her smiling through the phone as I talked to her, but I knew she was by the enraptured sound in her voice. She'd tell me she wish I was right there with her so she could hug and kiss me. Of course, that made me smile, too.

FIRST DEGREE LOVE

Being a "man of steal" means having to be one *on purpose*. Sometimes we need to premeditate or plan it in our palm pilots, calendars etc. whatever it takes to express to her that most needed affection. There is a satisfaction that runs very deep to the very core of us when we show affection to our wives. The feeling and experience is literally indescribable. This indescribable experience is a reward produced upon the genuine expression of affection. It brings back those great and wonderful, initial feelings you both had for each other in the beginning of your relationship. Some of you know exactly what I am talking about. It is one of those moments that are absolutely *priceless*.

Remember two things. 1) Your wife doesn't need a *Superman* (man of steel). She needs a *super man* (man of steal; a man of God). 2) Love your wife as Christ loved the church.

As the Lord Jesus instituted the "Lord's supper" or communion, we must institute a "marriage communion" or regular time to show our wives we love them. Jesus said of communion, "As often as you do it, you do show my death until I return," and we know His death shows love. For us husbands, let us say of our regular affection time with our wives, "As often as we do it, showing love and affection to our wives, we show it *until death do us part.*"

CHAPTER 4

Up, Up and Away!

One of the things that probably made Superman so cool was his ability to fly. I can't begin to count the number of times I dreamed I was flying, or wished I could really fly! I especially wished I could fly when I was only a kid. I think of all the times I could have just flew away. One day my mom gave me money to get a haircut after school. I'm not sure how this happened, but somewhere in between the time she gave it to me and the time I was supposed to get my haircut, I lost it. I lost $10! Yes, I wanted to just fly away.

Anyway, flying is a most desirable ability most people wish they had – not fly a plane, but to fly like Superman.

Well, I am here to serve notice to all my brothers that you can learn to fly today! How? You ask. No,

I'm not talking about literally flying, but flying away with your wife.

Consider the movie Superman. Remember the times Superman and Lois Lane were talking to each other, and then Lois Lane would step up on his boots, then they'd fly off, just the two of them – no one else. Is this starting to look like your honeymoon scene? This is the picture I am trying to create.

Recall your honeymoon. What two people were the highlight of your honeymoon? It was just the two of you, right? Remember how romantic it was, and fun, and almost beyond words. You sit back and wish it was always like that!

Well, see my fellow husbands, the two of you need to get away sometimes, and just focus on the two of you. Find someone to watch your kids. Make arrangements for a romantic getaway for two. Sometimes you need to just say good-bye to your job for about 3 days to a week. Yes, your wife is that important!

THOU SHALT DATE THY WIFE

You may ask, "What will we do? We're so used to the kids being around us. We may get bored." Well, that's the point of this getaway for the two of you. Like I said before, *make arrangements*, even on the things you will want to talk about. I know it sounds weird planning what you will talk about to a woman you already know. I mean, she's your wife for crying out loud.

However, ask yourself, "How well *do* I know my wife?" Ask yourself questions like these: What were the day, month and year of her conversion to Christ? When she first initially met me, what did she think of me? Did my breath smell good when we first kissed? Yes, these are simple questions, but they can lead to *profound conversations* and a deeper intimate relationship.

These questions are just models and stepping-stones to get you going in the right direction. Contrary to popular opinion, dating is good for married people. *The problem with a lot of marriages is that <u>dating is outdated</u>*. We need to bring dating back into our marriages.

Former pastor and Author of *The Christian Handbook for Pastors*, Kristofer Skrade lists in his book five ways to help your marriage thrive despite the demands of the being a pastor. Of those five, I will only mention one. He says, "Date your spouse: Schedule a time to enjoy fun activities or special places as a couple. Plan a surprise afternoon, evening, or weekend away with your spouse. If it helps, establish a weekly 'date night' and keep it religiously" (p. 202).

My wife and I attended what our church calls "Marriage Remix," lead by the Family and Adult Discipleship ministry department. One of the presenters told us a story my wife and I will never forget. The presenter, along with his wife, told us they created a regular dating schedule called "Naked Monday." Every Monday (and I'm not sure how they went about this exactly), they would get naked before each other and this was their official date night. (No, I don't know all they did, but do we really need to discuss that? Good. I didn't think so).

Now do you have that confused look on your face because I just told you married people should date? It's okay. Not only should they date, but should do it regularly. Well, before you become any more confused than you are already, let's define "dating," in the sense of two people not yet married to each other.

REMEMBER YOUR "GO OUT ON A DATE" DAY TO KEEP IT WHOLLY

First of all, many people define and describe dating differently. Some people define dating as a sin. Based on the way western culture, at large, dates, I would agree that it is sinful, too. The world's dating methods are not based upon scripture, but their own wisdom. The majority of western culture, as we know it, treats dating very seriously, like it *is* marriage. People have sex, in most cases, before the second time they meet for their next date. In most cases, these people never get married but live with each other like married people. Some of us know this as "shackin' up."

Of course, mainstream western culture uses dating based on the world's system – against God's way - this is not how I define dating. I should like to define dating as one lady phrased it: "Dating is not for mating, but for collecting data." Our culture uses dating for mating or having sex, but this isn't what it is for. As she said, it is for "collecting data," or getting to know the person you are dating.

I would add, extract information from your dating partner things that really matter – their faith and beliefs, their dreams, their goals, where they've been, where they're going, etc. Unfortunately, the questions we tend to ask are shallow, pointless and fleeting questions such as "How are you in the bedroom?" or "Ready to get your drink on?" or even "What kind of kisser are you?"

However, you're probably asking now, "How does all of this tie into me and my wife dating regularly? I'm glad you asked. First, get it out of your head that dating is a sin - because if it is, your marriage is doomed.

There is an old proverb that goes, "*Know* thyself." I have found in my few years of living that I am still getting to know myself – how I am, how I respond to different situations, how I tend to act around different kinds of people, etc. I am convinced it will take a lifetime to know myself.

To further make my point, let's use two excerpts from God's holy word, the Bible: the "trying of your faith," and "search me O God, try me, know my heart." These two excerpts from God's word are in direct reference to going through hard times and soul searching. Even more, one may think these passages say that God needs to find out what kind of person we are. Absolutely not!

The "trying of your faith" is not God allowing you to go through trials and tribulations so He can find out what you're really all about. Remember,

He already knows. He made us and created us. He knows all about us. The main part we miss is that He wants *us* "to know ourselves" through our hard times to become better people for Him.

So what is the connection about *knowing your own self* and dating your wife? Realizing that it takes all your life to know your own self, just imagine how long it would take to know someone else. Imagine someone who doesn't think exactly like you, had a different upbringing, different experiences, different personality, different ways of making decisions and so on and so on.

This is the exact picture of our marriages. You are married to a woman who is different than you. It is going to take a *lifetime* to know her. Our marriages will become better through getting to know each other – through something simple as dating.

So what's the concept? Date your wife! Take her out on dates. Get some alone time together, and make a point to do it regularly. I recall the words of Charles Stanley, "Children spell love T-I-M-E." And you know what? Wives spell it the same way. We all do. Anything worth while requires time. Is your wife worth your while? Of course she is! So take the time and get to know her *more*, treat her the way you used to or continue to treat her kindly, respectfully, and thoughtfully.

GIRLS JUST WANT TO HAVE FUN

Do you remember when you first met your wife? Do you remember how much fun you had? Recall all of those moments of joy and laughter. For some of us, fun has become desolate mainly due to the fact we don't date each other any more. All dates do not have to include $50 plates at some expensive restaurant every week. (Now that's no fun).

Allow me to throw out some ideas. For some of you who had your honeymoon at some special resort know of the things I'm about to say. You can go bowling, play basketball together, group date with another couple, ice-skate, get together with friends or just one another and play a board game like Taboo, Clue, Monopoly or Connect 4. The two of you could go site seeing in an area nearby that you haven't paid much attention to before. You could choose activities based on one of your interests or shared interests like renting a movie. You could even play interactive video games.

Well, as you can see, the possibilities are endless. The whole point being my brothers is that we have fun, and realize that she wants to have fun, too. You both need it actually. The Bible says that, "A merry heart does good like a medicine." You want a cure or healing for the desolation of fun in your marriage, plan fun things to do together!

Now notice in my suggestive list of fun things to do, I never mentioned lingerie and sex games. I purposely left that out because sometimes sex is *overrated*. If sex in and of itself were so fulfilling, why is it our wives don't always feel like being intimate in that way. Even those of us who have great marriages, our wives don't always feeling engaging in it. Heck, if we are honest with ourselves, we don't always feel like having sex.

Sex is not the only way married people have fun. Marriage isn't like a driver's license where you have sex because you can or are allowed to. Your marriage is bigger than sex! So you don't have to spice up your sex life! The crazy thing about sexual fulfillment is that it is experienced when you aren't even looking for it because you are focused on the entire spectrum of the marriage. The only reason we look for it or focus on it is because our culture, through lies and perversion, taught us to.

Don't get me wrong, though. If as a married couple you want to do sex games or kinky stuff, be my guest. Just make sure in all that you do that it glorifies Christ, doesn't defile your own conscience and that it is consensual between the two of you.

ROMANCE: IS IT GOD'S IDEA?

I should like to challenge our ideas of romance. It's more than roses, flowers, candy, elegant dates, first kisses, and opening the car door for your lady. It's more than walking her to her door to say goodnight, peering into her eyes as they reflect her beauty, or offering your coat to keep her warm in the park as the two of you take a night's stroll. It's even more than jewelry.

O my brothers, these things I just mentioned are fueled by something we often forget, neglect and underestimate. *We forget… to remember*; to be thoughtful.

Thoughtfulness is the power behind romance, and it is the thing we forget to do. Once upon a time, we reminded her of our love, but now we don't remind her any more. We make her do all the "guess work." She shouldn't have to guess, she should know. Just like we say in regards to living for Christ, "this is a <u>know-so</u> salvation." We *know* we are saved. We don't have to guess. In the same way, your wife should "know" she is special and important to you.

Now I must refer back to one of the modern writing prophets of whom I am inspired. Dr. Jimmy Evans says it best in his book, *Marriage on the Rock,* when he says,

> To help you understand where many marriages break down, think back to the first date with your spouse. <u>How hard did you work</u> at impressing your date? How much time did you spend preparing yourself physically? How careful were you with the words you spoke?
>
> How much energy did you exert serving and trying to please your date? You know as well as I do that <u>we all "broke our necks" trying to impress each other on the first date.</u>
>
> This shows clearly that it was not simply "chemistry" that caused your relationship to be so satisfying at the start. It also Involved a lot of hard work. One normally works very hard at a relationship until one is secure in the love of the other person. <u>When the relationship seems secure, one gradually reduces</u>

the effort and begins to take it for granted (p. 35).

Romance has always been fueled by a lot of hard work, or as I put it, thoughtfulness. We put a lot of thought into what we did. *We must remember to remember* (or to be thoughtful). In another book that I wrote, I said, "We are creatures of forgetfulness, but memory is a skill." And any skill requires practice. So yes, romance *is* God's idea, but before you can be romantic, you must *remember*... or... *be thoughtful*. To further prove it, let's check out Ecclesiastes 12:1.

It reads, "Remember now your Creator in the days of your youth." (Refer Phil. 4:8 and chapter 2 – X-Ray Vision).

Yes, again you probably say, "This scripture is pertaining to God, not my wife." Again I say to you, see the principle the scripture teaches. Let us first look at the word "remember." When it says "remember," it isn't just talking about "bringing something to mind for the sheer joy of it and then let it pass as quickly as it came." This kind of remembrance produces results. It brings about action. It requires you to do something.

Recall the thief on the cross who said to Jesus, "Lord, *remember* me when You come into Your kingdom." Jesus' response to him was, "Today you shall be with me in Paradise." See! The man wasn't just asking Jesus to have him in his mind as a passing thought. He was asking Jesus to actually *do* something for him – in his case, to obtain forgiveness.

In the case with this scripture in Ecclesiastes 12, the writer is encouraging young people to *do things* for God while they are still young. In this case, remembrance produces obedience to God. Notice in the last verses in Ecclesiastes 12. It says, "The conclusion, when all has been heard, is: fear God and keep His commandments." So see, the young remember so to obey God.

So when we, husbands, remember, the end result is romance. She will say before the night is over, "O, he's so romantic!" She will say this because of your presentation or special delivery of your deed of kindness to her. But you may say, "My life is too busy to be romantic all the time." Well, I didn't say be romantic, even though it is God's idea. I said "Remember." All it takes is five minutes a day to do something thoughtful, considerate and nice for her. This takes us back to other portions of this book that teach us to show our wives we are thinking about them and that we love them. (Refer to chapter 3 Man of Steel/Steal).

She is your priority. Never let yourself be too busy to show her love. "Custom love" your wife. If she doesn't like flowers or roses or are allergic to them, don't bring them to her. You'd do more harm than good. Bring her something "she" likes and isn't allergic to.

For some of us who need another word for "romance" because we define it by the world's standards, let me use this word instead: ROYAL REMEBRANCE.

How to be a Super Man to your Wife

We treat our wives like royalty (like a queen) by putting a lot of thought into loving her. Consider this: *Husbands, don't be a king over your wife, instead treat her like a queen.*

After hearing all I have shared in this passage, let me leave you with one final thought as I close this chapter.

Do you recall the song "I believe I can fly?" Well, if you don't recall this song, let me give you some of the lyrics: *I believe I can fly, I believe I can touch the sky. I think about it every night and day, spread my wings and fly away. I believe I can soar, see me running through that open door. I believe I can fly.*

Well, I told you in the beginning of this chapter that you possessed the ability to fly away with your wife. Do you believe you can fly? See, there are many married men who "think about it ("it" being the joy of marriage, and wanting to have it with their wives, but don't have it) every night and day."

My brothers, you do not have to keep thinking about it. You can actually fly away with your wife! You can bring back those days of dating, romance (royal remembrance) and fun. Just see yourself running through the open door. It's open! Don't wait for the perfect time. My former pastor once said, "The tragedy of waiting for the perfect time is that there *is* no perfect time. There is only an accepted time," which is *right now*. The best time is *now*…right now! Make it happen and as Nikey says, "Just do it."

CHAPTER 5

He Who has Ears to Hear, Let him Hear

In the movie *Superman Returns*, Superman visits Lois Lane so she can interview him. Then, after all her questions, Superman asks her to accompany him high in the sky. Now as they both are suspended in the sky, he poses a question to her. "What do you hear?" She responds, "Nothing." He comes back. "I hear everything."

Superman's super-hearing ability made him really sensitive to those in need or in trouble. It put him in touch with those in danger. It made him accessible to help numerous people. It's like he had a built-in scanner picking up all earthly activity.

This ability to hear is a big part of what made Superman *Superman*. For us, it isn't any different. If our marriages are to radiant God's glory, we are going to have to listen to our wives more *attentively* and *intentionally*. We need to tune into her.

Whenever Superman would retreat to the sky to listen to what was going on in the world, he had to be in the right place to hear it. For instance, have you ever been driving and listening to your favorite radio program and suddenly you reach a dead spot or tunnel where the radio signal is lost or blocked? Isn't that the most annoying thing? Well, the signal is lost or blocked because you are not in the right position to hear it.

Now before I continue on this important ability we're to have, let me briefly explain the difference between "hearing" and "listening," because you can hear without listening *but* you cannot listen unless you can hear.

Hearing is *involuntary* and listening is *voluntary*. Hearing requires the right position while listening requires focus and concentration.

For example, if you attend a family get-together, you will *involuntarily hear* many of your family members talking to one another, and you won't be listening to everything they are saying. It's like being in a crowd of people. You *hear* voices but no words. Now listening means just the opposite. At some point you make a point to really *voluntarily listen* to the words you hear. There is reception and feedback on your part. Someone says something and you are able to speak or respond to what you heard and listened to.

Someone says, for example, 'Those are the best chips on the market!' You, then could respond, 'O yeah, are you talking about those Pringles?" However, you can't give feedback on something you have not listened or tuned into.

Fellow husbands, it isn't any different being married. If you aren't tuned into your wife, or listening to her, you will find your own life robbed of peace. It will be so annoying that even when she is making a sensible point, but because you aren't in tuned with her, will be pure static. You'll be unable to receive her signals. Even worse, arguments are birthed in such atmospheres where the two of you aren't tuned into one another. A big part of living together is actively listening to one another and living beyond your *own* world and thoughts.

Now just in case you're wondering what the 'right' and 'wrong' positions for being in tuned with your wife are, let me share a few with you. First, the right positions include praying together and communicating regularly with each other. You both need not only speak with each other, but also speak your heart to each other. Be open with each other. Don't hide things from her. Even those things you think you *shouldn't* share with her, share them. Every detail matters. Of course, avoid morbid details. There *is* such a thing as *too much information*. Remember, too, that she isn't just your girlfriend anymore. She is your wife. You have an obligation to her. It is the kind of obligation that should be governed by joy, gladness and willingness, not grudgingly, or out of compulsion.

The wrong positions include things such as watching TV as she is trying to bond and connect with you, especially if you know TV throws off your reception when your wife is trying to talk to you. When I talk to my wife, I ensure that the TV isn't on. I can't focus on what she is saying to me, and then I end up giving her the short end of the stick. So when we talk, we do so with the TV off. Or maybe you try to bond with your wife while your buddies are around. Absolutely not! Your bonding time is done alone – just the two of you. Wrong positioning also includes not praying together and communicating regularly.

I recall the words of my College Pastor, Rev. Melvin Jenkins, saying, "We must be *active listeners*." What he meant was that we must be intentional about listening or about what we hear. It is *listening* on purpose *or* tuning into what the other person is saying. In this case, it is our wives.

Here is a Biblical principle to help us understand "active listening." The Bible says in James 1:19, "Be *slow to speak* and *swift to hear, slow to anger*." So in regards to your wife, don't be so eager to speak your mind, but let her speak hers. Be more reluctant to speak until you have heard her speak her whole heart to you.

I mean, let's say the two of you are having some issues. How can you resolve them when you've only heard a fourth of what she's trying to say due to your anxiousness to speak? You can't. So be patient and *just* listen. Notice the verse says, "slow to anger." If you are slow to speak, you will be swift to hear, and most likely not get angry and completely avoid an argument. So the mandate to be good hearers and listeners are absolutely critical for our marriages.

CLEARING THE AIR

Before I met my wife, I was dating a girl, who, whenever I told her she didn't listen to me, thought I was saying that she didn't obey me – you know, to listen as a child does to his/her own parent(s). To her, the word "listen" meant, "obey." To me, all it meant was "hear me as I speak so you won't misunderstand me."

Now I shared this brief story for those of you who thought I was telling you to "take orders" from your wife. I hope through my short story you have learned what I mean when I say "listen." A husband, contrary to "the devil's opinion," is *not* required to obey his wife. (*And while we're on the subject, wives aren't supposed to obey their husbands. Only children under the care of their parents are to obey – you, the husband and your wife*). And I know we joke around and say we're supposed to obey her, but that's a lie. The only one we obey is God. The Bible mandates us to love our wives as Christ loved the church. This love moves us to serve her *just as if* we do obey her.

BREAKING THE BARRIER OF MISCOMMU-NICATION

Romans 8:26 says, "The Spirit helps our weaknesses. We don't know what to pray for as we ought to, but the Spirit intercedes for us to the Father with groans that cannot be spoken."

God always understands us completely. How? He understands completely because, as the next verse says (v. 27), He knows the mind of the Spirit who speaks on our behalf. It's another way of saying He knows how the Spirit thinks perfectly. They understand each other totally. So God can never misunderstand us. There are no barriers to us communicating with Him. Also, as the Bible says, "God looks at and knows our hearts." And might I add, He knows our hearts perfectly.

Remember that we are talking about communication with our wives. As we did in earlier chapters, extracting the principles from Scripture, let's use the term "pray" in Romans 8:26 as our wives talking to us.

Some of us usually describe our wives as "nagging." When she speaks to us, it's always about what we *aren't* doing. It's like you can't do enough good things. You can be enjoying a nice movie together, and "out of nowhere," she says something like, "Why don't you treat me like that?" And it's not like she says this every now and then. She says things like that very often. So often does she do it, you wish you could mute every word that came out of her mouth the moment she starts *just* to keep yourself from getting upset or angry.

While her nagging is, indeed, irritating, I need us to see her nagging as the "groanings" mentioned in Romans 8:26. Think of her nagging as a *bad way* of expressing what's in her heart and mind. As God looks past our "bad ways" or sins and looks at our hearts, let us look past the "nagging" or *bad ways* of our wives, and see her heart. She has a real concern, but she's just going about it the wrong way. Leave some margin for error.

Now you're probably thinking that our wives, if they do nag us to death, should stop and check themselves. If you *are* thinking this, know that this is true. She should check herself *but* this book is called *How to be a Super Man to your wife*, not *How to focus on your wife's actions*. The focus is on us – on husbands.

Now I know we've been told that all men have an "mute switch" or an "internal on/off switch," where we ignore our wives and tune them out because of all the nagging they're doing to us. We usually laugh and joke about our "internal on/off switch," but it is no laughing matter. Tapping into our "internal on/off switch" against the nagging of our wives will not allow us to see her heart. So here are a few tangible steps to help hear her heart should she begin "nagging."

ASSUME THE POSITION

The first step is to treat her nagging words as words in which to judge yourself. *Assume the position* you are wrong even though you do not believe you are. You never know. You just may be. Her nagging may contain some truth. Jesus said, "You shall know the truth, and it will make you free." So do not dismiss what she's saying entirely. Don't be on the defensive justifying yourself, nor "switching her off," but as I said, judging yourself. Consider that she *just* might be right and you may very well be wrong. The Bible also says, "the one who says they have no sin lies and the truth is not in such a person." A more up-dated way of saying this scripture is "Nobody's perfect," and we're no exception to the rule.

Before I get to the next step, *I will* admit it *is* hard to hear the heart of your wife when she is nagging. But my dear brothers, the mere fact we point out she is nagging (and here is the next step), we tattletale on ourselves. How? Because a nagging wife is usually the byproduct of a disengaged husband. This kind of husband usually doesn't set up times for he and his wife to spend a romantic evening together. He isn't fun. He's boring and always caught up in his work or always hanging out with his buddies. He's a married man trying to live like he's single.

Dr. Jimmy Evans says in his book, "…Because a wife is dependent upon her husband for leadership and provision, she naturally will respond to what her husband does and does not do. The reason is that, in the beginning, God created Adam to be the initiator and Eve to <u>reflect</u> Adam's glory as his helpmate and companion." In other words, maybe *we* are the reason she is nagging. We nag her by our indifferent attitude toward her. Unfortunately, she returns irritation for irritation, *or* we're just reaping what we've sown. It could also be due to the fact that we neglect to communicate with her on a regular basis.

Third and lastly, keep in mind that *nagging reveals your marital needs*. The marital need in this case is putting her first. It's an annoying way of saying what your marriage needs in order to be strong. So I again, encourage us not to be so quick to jump on the defensive on the onset of nagging. It's more a blessing in disguise than we actually realize, namely because it's not really "nagging." Her words only *become* nagging because we aren't in tuned to her. We're selfish!

Again, we don't put her in her rightful place. We make ourselves the first human priority. When she isn't the first human priority, *anything* she says will be annoying and nagging. Ultimately, she is fighting for her rightful place, and this is what her heart cries out for.

I, again, would like to borrow from one of the modern writing prophets of my day. Dr. Jimmy Evans says on the subject of priority, "To put it simply, God designed marriage to operate as the second most important priority in life, coming next to your relationship with Him. If we put marriage in any position of priority other than the one God has instituted, the marriage does not work" (Marriage on the Rock, p. 20).

THOU SHALT HAVE NO ONE ELSE BEFORE HER

For a minute, let's visit the words of Jesus in Luke 14:26. He says, "You cannot come with Me unless you love Me more than you love your own life" (CEV). We are not worthy of Jesus unless He is first, and loved more than anyone in our lives. I only quoted a portion of verse 26 of Luke 14, but if you read the whole verse in your Bible, you will find that this even means…your wife.

Now some of us have heard of the J.O.Y. principle. J for Jesus first, O for Others second and Y for Yourself last. Focus on the O for Others. Do you know who the first O would be for us husbands? You guessed it. Our wives! If you truly want joy in your marriage (and life), put your wife before everyone, except God of course. Make time for her. Listen to her heart and I guarantee you she won't sound like a "noisy gong or clanging cymbal."

BABY BOY GENERATION

Some of us are familiar with the movie *Baby Boy*. However, for those of you who aren't, let me give you a brief overview. *Baby Boy* is about an young African-American who won't "fly out of the nest." And anyone who knows anything about the way eagles raise their young, at some point, their young must leave the nest. More importantly, the way the mother eagle sends her young out of the nest, she basically kicks them out. In other words, it would be unnatural and imbalanced for a baby eagle to stay with its mother when it's time for it to go. It will never grow to be the eagle it was intended to be.

Well, anyway, the boy wouldn't leave home because he was afraid. Even though he had two kids of his own, still, he wouldn't leave. He still wanted his mom to take care of him, even as a grown man!

Herein lies the problem for most marriages. Most married men never "left" their mom and "cleaved" to their wife (Genesis 2:24). There is a transition of priority that must take place in order for a marriage to grow strong. A better way to say this would be "Your wife comes before your parents," or "Wifey before Mommy." Our moms must come second to our wives. If she doesn't, as Dr. Evans said, don't expect your marriage to work.

Now don't get me wrong. I am not encouraging you to stop loving your mom and appreciating all she has done for you. Please know that I am not saying that at all – not by a long shot. I can't think of a man who loves and appreciates his mom more than I.

The truth of the matter is that most men grow very close to their moms very early in their lives. However, we must be careful not to allow our closeness with our mothers to interfere with our relationship with our wives. Now notice that I <u>*didn't*</u> say, "We mustn't get close to our moms..." By all means, get close to your mom, but just make sure your wife comes first. My brothers, don't be afraid to take this most crucial step. It is God-ordained. This isn't just some advice I'm handing out because I heard someone say it on TV one day. So let him who has ears to hear, hear what the Spirit says.

CHAPTER 6

Step Fathers, Step *Farther*

I reserved this section of the book for husbands who are step dads. I believe that there is a special grace given to such men. They love and embrace children who aren't their biological children. However, I haven't written this section to teach parenting skills for the step dad. I have written this section to teach step dads how to treat the biological father of your children. We must step out farther, beyond loving our step kids. Respect the man *they* come from.

Again, recall Superman from *Superman Returns*. When he returned back from his planet, Krypton, he came back and discovered that his only love, Lois Lane, now was with another man! Ouch! Who'd ever think that of all people Superman would find himself in such a situation? Nevertheless, Superman showed him kindness and respect.

Well, for many of us, it is just the same. We've found ourselves with step kids and dealing with the father of those kids who are now yours too.

Be encouraged my fellow super men. I am one of many men who fall into this category. Let me share with you some words of wisdom or helpful tips in dealing with the biological father (bio dad) of your children and give you a new perspective.

Going back to chapter 2, praising your wife is the first step. Our fear, at times, is that our wife is going to leave us for *bio dad*. Sadly, there are songs implanted in our minds with subliminal messages. They teach us that our wife is subject to go back with *bio dad* (baby mama drama kind of stuff) – that she still has feelings for him and is thinking about getting together with him.

Listen! Get that nonsense out of your head! That is just the enemy playing musical lies! Don't give Satan opportunities to perform his orchestrated lies. Letting your wife know of the wonderful things she does turns her attention toward you. Know that by doing so, she won't have time to think about *bio dad*. As we established earlier, "women blossom in an atmosphere of praise." So even when *bio dad* comes over to see his kids, she won't give him a second thought, much less a "first" thought.

You say, "But what if *bio dad* praises her, too?" If you say it, it won't mean anything if he does. Praise needs to come from you, the husband. And when it does, she will be satisfied and content. If *bio dad* should praise your wife in some way, when he does do it, it will only validate *your words*. She won't see his praise as supplements, just a compliment. God gave <u>you</u> to your wife, and <u>only you</u> can meet all of those marital needs. No one else can, and no one else is supposed to.

The next step I highly recommend is *making known your presence*. I also call this the *principle of presence*. In other words, don't *disappear* when bio dad *appears*. Remember that your wife is *your wife*. She belongs to you, not bio dad. Neither one of you (between you and bio dad) should feel uncomfortable around each other, but if either of you should be uncomfortable or walking on eggshells, it should be bio dad.

Now when we are in church, we usually sing songs or praise God with this praise: *God, make your presence known to your people*. Right? Okay, so what is so significant about this praise? It is that there is power in His presence. His presence makes the difference. We say in His presence, demons have got to go and miracles begin to happen. My brothers, I just want to serve notice on you that *our presence* has power too.

Don't feel awkward being around your own wife just because bio dad is around. Don't force your presence either, but when the opportunity presents itself, be there. If necessary, bring yourself into the conversation. Ask questions and be equally engaged as your wife and bio dad talks. Again, keep in mind that she is *your wife*! Now between you and your wife, there shouldn't be any place the two of you can't follow each other.

Hopefully she knows this because the *principle of presence* is twice as effective when she *doesn't* exclude you.

As we sing the song to God: *You are welcome in this place*, I hope your wives do the same in welcoming you into every part of their lives. Even if they don't do this, make sure you exemplify it yourself since you are the head, the initiator. We lead by example. In the meanwhile, pray for your wife that she welcome your presence everywhere in her life, especially around bio dad.

R-E-S-P-E-C-T

The last step or principle I would like to share is politeness and respect. In a nutshell, we need to be polite to bio dad. Disrespecting him will only backfire on you. When we aren't polite to bio dad, we open the door for our wives to jump to his defense. Soon after that, we run the big, big chance of accusing our wife of "marital" treason for taking his side instead of ours.

Remember that it's not you (the step dad) vs. bio dad. Your enemy is the devil and your own insecurities. The two of you (you and bio dad) actually work together for the welfare of his child(ren), at least you should be anyway.

As I think about it, I recall an incident in my life where, once upon a time, I was dating a girl. Two months later, we broke up. Then three months later, I met another girl who knew the girl I'd just broken up with. One day we were going to eat at the college cafeteria, and we ran into my ex. My new girlfriend insisted we sit with my ex and my ex's friends. Honestly brothers, I just wasn't ready for this.

I did my best to explain to my new girlfriend that I didn't want to sit with my ex. Not understanding why I didn't want to, she started accusing me of wanting to get back together with my ex, and that I wasn't completely over her and all that stuff. There'd even be times where my new girlfriend would say some "out-of-line" things about my ex due to her own insecurities. I, then, found myself defending my ex from my new girlfriend.

My point for this story is to show the backfiring effect of disrespecting bio dad because of your own insecurities. You create a great chance of your wife defending bio dad, which will only deepen your insecurities. And the deeper you go into your insecurities, you will open the door for Satan to feed you more lies.

Your wife, however, will not feel inclined to protect bio dad if you are showing him politeness and kindness. Quite the contrary, she will be on your side.

For your amusing pleasure and learning, here is an incident that happened to me before my wife and I married. It seemed that upon asking my wife to marry me, all the guys who liked her were coming out of the woodworks looking to "get with her." I would hate it sometimes when she told me these guys would call. (Of course, as I look back, I'm glad she did share it with me. It showed me she loved me and respected me).

So this one particular guy who was pursuing her stopped by to see her and I was there this day. Now previous to his arrival, at least a few days before, I asked Jasmine about his welfare because he had been shot and put in the hospital.

While he was over her house this day, he asked a question that showed his awkardness of my presence. Jasmine responded to him a tad indignantly, "He asked about you." He, then, turned to me, and thanked me for my concern.

See the principle of politeness in my story? My respect for him and politeness made my wife feel at ease. So instead of having to defend him (had I been disrespectful or impolite), she defended me instead. When she defended me, it produced respect in him to show it to me.

BONUS CHAPTER

HUSBANDS IN WAITING

When you are waiting for your wife, you need not nag her and say, "Hurry up baby, we're late!" If you know anything about women, you know rushing them to hurry up is mission: impossible. It's futile to even try.

There are times I tell my kids to wait when they want to watch TV. This sounds innocent enough to say but they take it *literally*. They will actually sit on the steps and just wait, doing nothing. Mind you, I never told them how long they would have to wait. So after two minutes, naturally, they ask again, "Can I watch TV?"

I respond, "No. Didn't I tell you to wait?" Of course, they respond, "Yes." So one day, I got smart by the grace of God. I explained to them that waiting involved doing something while they waited to watch TV. They could either read a book or play their games until I told them they could watch TV.

So I try to encourage them to do something super fun. This way, they will be so preoccupied and engaged in what they're doing that they won't even think about watching TV until I call them downstairs.

Even Jesus said to us as believers, "Occupy until I come." There were some believers in the Apostle Paul's day who were waiting for the return of Christ, but they literally were waiting without occupying themselves with the things of God. This is sinful to do. The Bible also says, "He that knows to do good and doesn't do it, he is sinning."

Husbands, I give us the mandate to do the same. If your wife is running late, do not complain or rush her, just occupy yourself. Here are some things you can do. First, see what you can do to help her *hurry along*.

We must be like Jesus who said, "I didn't come to be served, but to serve." Philippians 2:5 says, "Let this mind be in you – the same mind Christ had…who emptied Himself and took the *form of a servant*…" You must take on the mind or mentality of a servant. She becomes the queen and you are the lowly servant.

Maybe she needs you to take something out of the dryer for her or iron some clothes. *Rushing* her is like that scripture in the Bible that says, "Which of you by worrying can add 18 inches to your height?" You will only frustrate yourself if you actually try to rush your wife out of the house or store. So I ask us, "Who among us can make her move any faster through complaining and a bad attitude?"

Another thing you could do is tidy up the car, or if it's cold outside, go warm up the car. The idea is to keep yourself busy until she is ready. You can also apply these concepts to those times that you and your wife are shopping in the mall or grocery store.

Say, for example, you are a husband who is married with children. If you can't stand shopping with your wife, use this time to spend it with the kids. Catch up on the current events of their lives. Take the time to play with them. Keep in mind, though, that kids tend to get a little out of control, so play with them in moderation.

Now on the flip side of her running late, I encourage the two of you to set aside a time to sit down and discuss the problem of always running late. The two of you may decide to do things the night before so to make the next day "smooth sailing." *Occupation breeds optimism.* If you think positively, you will repel a negative demeanor and countenance and nagging on your part. You will most definitely keep an *intense fellowship* from occurring. God desires that you and your wife have peace woven in the fabric of your marriage.

CONCLUSION

Why Our Wives Need A Super Man

Like Lois Lane did to Superman, for many of us, our wives have written us off, too. Maybe they haven't officially endorsed hopelessness for the both of you, but she may be pondering it even as you read this.

Superman was in the same exact situation as you are. When he came back and saw the article Lois Lane wrote, *Why the World doesn't need Superman*, he was really devastated. He believed the two of them had something special, but obviously, whatever was so special that they shared was not strong enough to keep her from writing that article.

See my brothers, the thing of it is if we do not step up to be the Bible living husbands God is calling for, we sell our marriages short. God designed our wives for nothing short of a godly man. Being a super man isn't really an option for us. Either we will be or not be.

Now here is the turning point for you if your marriage is spiraling downward. Upon Superman's return, he was really doing some super things, eventually stopping Lex Luther from taking over the world. Superman gave Lois Lane a reason to write *another* article: *Why the world needs Superman.*

We must give our wives a reason to put away hopeless thoughts about the survival of our marriage. Again, step up and be a super man and do super things, or step up and be a Bible living husband who acts in the best interest of his wife.

All that I mentioned in this book: drawing your strength from the Son (reading God's word and prayer); using your X-ray vision (praising and appreciating your wife); being a man of steal (show her genuine affection), flying away together (date and remember her) and listening if you have ears to hear (listen to her heart). Respect your step kids' biological father, and keep yourself busy as she gets ready. If we commit to doing these things, we will prove ourselves to be real super men.

Closing Prayer

Heavenly Father in the name of Jesus, I pray that the words spoken in this book will speak to the readers. May the principles of Your glorious divine truth permeate the very core of us. May what we've read not fall on deaf ears.

Having read this book, don't let us leave the same way we came. Let us be able to sing, "I won't leave here like I came in Jesus' name – bound, afflicted, sick or lame. For the Spirit of the Lord is still the same. I won't leave here like I came in Jesus' name."

May the blessings You have in stored for the married, taste of Your goodness and experience the wonderful design of marriage, and its joy. Lord Jesus, it's in your name we pray, Amen.

www.ingramcontent.com/pod-product-compliance
Ingram Content Group UK Ltd.
Pitfield, Milton Keynes, MK11 3LW, UK
UKHW041944230426
12048UKWH00008B/114